ROMAN BRI

A History From Beginning To End

BY

HENRY FREEMAN

Table of Contents

Introduction

From its beginning on April 21st 753 BCE, Rome gradually expanded its foundation and power structure to become the center of an Empire—indisputably one of the greatest, most tumultuous of empires in human history. Under the guidance of rulers from Romulus to Emperor Romulus Augustus, Rome and its eventual Empire spanned a little over one thousand years. Inevitably, given their relatively close proximity to present-day Italy, the British Isles would feel the tendrils of Rome creeping ever nearer. But would those tendrils ever take as firm a hold as the roots that were put down in Rome itself?

The answer, much to Rome and her emperors' chagrin, was no. That did not stop them from trying, however, and try they did - long and hard - to maintain stability in the provinces that constituted Britannia. Yet never was there an easy peace to be had. Always there was an air of malaise, a feeling of unrest among the native population. Perhaps there was reason for it; perhaps there was unruliness for unruliness' sake. No one will ever know the dialogues between the first Romans to visit and the peoples they found there. One can imagine the shock that must have passed between them, though.

It was 55 BCE when Julius Caesar invaded the island of Britain for the first time as part of the Gallic Wars. This was due to the fact that the Britons were believed to be helping the Roman enemy, the Gauls, in what is present-day France. In the decades following Caesar's success,

Emperor Augustus attempted to return thrice, but each invasion was cancelled. Caligula's men, almost a century after Caesar's invasions, gathered on the Gallic side of the Channel but never made it across. Finally, in 43 CE, Emperor Claudius sent four legions to the island to restore an exiled king over the Atrebas tribe there. The general consensus is that the Romans officially had a foothold on the Isle by 47 CE, still under Claudius' rule.

In the second century CE, two great walls were constructed on account of the general unrest between Romans and native Britons. Around 197 CE the Severan reforms divided Britannia into two provinces; by the third century the Diocletian Reforms made two more provinces, and in the fourth century a fifth and final province was added. Not long after, by 410 CE at the latest, Roman control was withdrawn from Britannia forever. With nearly four-hundred and sixty years of rule over the island, the Romans undoubtedly changed the shape of the land and the structure of the people there.

Growth is inevitable, but what about the clashes? The conflicts? There were certainly plenty of those as well. This book will lay out the timeline before diving into the issues of Celtic identity, the task of actually getting to Britain, the blending of culture with religion as an example once the Romans arrived, and finally the withdrawal from the island as the Roman Empire began its decline.

Chapter One

The Timeline

The 43 CE invasion of the island of Britannia was led by Aulus Plautius. It was deemed a success by the Emperor Claudius back in Rome. Future Emperor Vespasian commanded one of the legions. This was actually a common practice; a number of future Emperors got their start with military experience on the "frontiers" of the Roman Empire. Two battles were required to defeat the Catuvellani tribe of southeast England and their allies. The first was on the river Medway and the other was on the river Thames. Elephants may have been involved. The Catuvellani leader, Togodumnus, was killed and a man by the name of Cogidubnus was installed as the new king. Yet Caratacus, the brother of Togodumnus, did not react well to the disposal of his kin. Caratacus became a sort of resistance leader and faced the Romans again in 51 CE. The Roman governor of Britannia at the time, Publius Ostorius Scapula, was able to defeat Caratacus; the loser fled to the Brigantes in the north where he thought he could find safety in the hills. However, the Brigantes' queen Cartimandua had other ideas, and she turned Caratacus over to Rome.

Between 60 and 61 CE the tribes of Britannia had another resistance leader emerge from the depths. Boudica, the widow of the Iceni king Prasutagus, rose in rebellion against Governor Gaius Suetonius Paulinus. After Prasutagus' death, the king had left half of his kingdom to the Roman Emperor at the time, Nero, and half to his wife and daughters. However, Rome was not satiated by this offering and took the rest of the kingdom for her own - because she could. The Iceni, joined by the Trinovantes, marched on Camulodunum (present-day Colchester), Londinium (London), and Verulamium (St. Albans) and destroyed all three cities. They were finally defeated at the Battle of Watling Street, and Boudica herself died shortly after. The circumstances of her death are unclear.

69 CE was the "year of four emperors" in quick succession: Galba, Otho, Vitellius, and Vespasian. After Nero's suicide in 68 CE, Rome witnessed a short stretch of civil war, and three different faces on the throne, before Vespasian settled in for a while. This left the Roman legions in Britannia restless. Cartimandua, the Brigantes' queen who turned Caratacus over to Rome and who was now living under Roman protection herself, was chased out of the northern reaches of the province by Venutius, a more loyal member of the Brigantes—loyal to his tribe, as opposed to having loyalty to the Emperor and Rome.

In what is present-day Scotland, the Caledonii tribe ran amok, in the opinion of the Romans. The Battle of Mons Graupius, which took place in 84 CE, was a landmark victory for Governor Gnaeus Julius Agricola and his men. This was after his conquering of the Ordovices in 78 CE as well. Shortly after, though, he was called back to Rome, and in Rome he would die. Fast forward to 105 CE and the Picts of Alba were causing more trouble in the north. After so much "progress" under Governor Agricola, the Romans had begun to lose ground.

The duty of the governors in Rome was to run imperial provinces. They were also members of the Senate. Whereas the Senate controlled peaceful provinces, it was up to the Emperor to control garrisons and things of war. The Legatus Juridicus was the governor's legal advisor, and the Procurator dealt with financial administration. Various commanders answered to the Governor when it came to military actions, of which there were many. The Roman Empire was very militaristic of course, with the idea being to expand its borders as much as realistically possible.

In 117 CE Emperor Hadrian's reign began. His name might sound familiar, for he ordered the construction of one of the gigantic walls in northern England. When he made it up to Britain in around 120 CE he directed the building of a wall on the edge of the Stanegate frontier below Scotland. The Antonine Wall was built around 142 CE by another second century emperor even further north of Hadrian's Wall. The unrest from the north must have been palpable to dictate the construction of such massive formations. From 155 to 157 CE, the Brigantes revolted in Scotland. The Antonine Wall was (unfortunately for the Romans) abandoned, recaptured a year later, and then completely abandoned by 164 CE.

With all this talk about Catuvellani and Brigantes, Iceni and Trinovantes, Caledonians and Picts, where are the "Celts" of fame? The next chapter will examine the difficulties archaeologists and historians face when attempting to label ancient peoples with umbrella terms like "Celt" or "Celtic".

Chapter Two

Ancient Celtic Ethnicity, A Modern Invention

When someone mentions "ancient Britain" an image of a green, fertile island—complete with coastal cliffs and dark forests shrouded in mist—may be what comes to mind. Perhaps a mystical Druid wanders through the forest in your head; maybe it's a woad-painted warrior Celt. There are hill forts perched on grassy mountaintops and sparring tribes. But what about when someone says "Roman Britain"? Perhaps you think of towering stone walls and straight roads, impressive aqueducts and hot spring baths. You would be mostly correct about both. The only questionable thought is the labeling of your woad-painted warrior a "Celt".

So who, then, did the Romans encounter on the British Isles if not the Celts? The answer is more complex than one may have been led to believe previously. Too many groups of peoples existed on the island of Britannia at the time when Romans were first making contact for those peoples to easily fall under the umbrella category of Celtic; some lists include twenty-seven disparate tribes, to give an example of how varied the situation was. [1] In order to interpret and absorb the full "Roman Britain" picture it is first essential to understand the nature of the native Briton. Let's start by clarifying the use of the term "Celtic".

The question "what is Celtic?" is difficult to answer. In the modern day, phrases like "Celtic music", "Celtic dancing", and "Celtic languages" are quite common. They are used to evoke an earlier, mystical time and a proud, historical people; in addition to these evocations, one can generally assume that the person who is speaking of such "Celtic" things is referring to the inhabitants of the British Isles. The reality, though, is very different. In exploring the question it becomes evident that the term "Celtic" did not gain popularity until the eighteenth century, and even then the word was misapplied and the definition misconstrued: reality shows that those cultural things like music, dancing, and language that people would consider today to be part of "ancient Celtic ethnicity" are in fact part of a fairly modern invention that arises from a people actually originating on the continent of Europe. [2]

Vincent and Ruth Megaw wrote in their 1996 criticism of Malcolm Chapman that even though the name "Keltoi" was applied by the Greeks to non-Greeks or "Others", this incorrect—according to Chapman—naming "does not prove the fictitious nature of the Celts, just as the limited, Eurocentric, 18th -century perceptions of the First Australians do not mean there were no people in 'Australia' before European contact, nor that all of the observations made on the early voyages were inaccurate". [3] Another example of this would be Christopher Columbus naming the Native Americans he encountered "Indians" simply because he did not know that he had not, indeed, found his way to the East Indies. The Megaws would say that even though the name "Indian" was erroneously given, that does not make the notes which were subsequently taken about these people's untrue. The same could be said about the Greeks and Romans and their encounters with the "Celts" or "Gauls". Even though those Celts or Gauls did not refer to themselves as Celtic or Gallic until the eighteenth century, in the Megaws' eyes it is not necessarily a bad thing nowadays to refer to those ancient people by such names. [4]

The Megaws fall into dangerous territory, however, when they attempt to do just this, or in other words, when they try to group these Celts from the ancient world into one neatly packaged ethnic group. Many, like Simon James, argue that there are too many differences in culture—the arts, religion, and language—to be able to group together the varied peoples originating around the same time period, specifically the Iron Age. [5] The grouping of ancient people due to their association with La Tène culture, for instance, officially became troublesome due to Joseph Déchelette's book on archaeology. It was he who first associated La Tène with the ancient Celtic individual, and his oversimplified analysis of burial sites were, in the words of John Collis, "dubious in the extreme." [6] Déchelette thought it possible to chart ethnicities based on the way people in a certain area were buried, and so he followed the expansion of the Celts on a map and believed himself to have found corresponding burial sites in the same areas of Celtic expansion. The Megaws are two of those individuals who claim that La Tène art is evidence of a solid Celtic culture group, and it is Collis who realizes the potential danger in applying a name to an ethnicity based on archaeology. [7]

According to Collis, "ancient usage [of 'Celt' and 'Gaul'] is not consistent" between ancient authors in their time, which makes pinning down one ethnicity quite difficult. [8] In the sixth-century BCE one first finds mention of a "Keltoi" people so-named by the Greeks. [9] These people originated north of the Alps sometime between 800 BCE and 600 BCE. [10] Michael Dietler wrote, "The Celts thus became, for the Mediterranean world, the first alien people on their northern border to emerge out of the mists of prehistory with a seemingly coherent identity." [11] This identity spread across the continent of Europe and to the British Isles, but there was no "mass migration" of these people to the Isles or invasion of the Isles like some have claimed. [12] It seems to have been a more gradual spread of culture across the English Channel where the identity still resides today.

What then of "modern Celticism"? And how exactly did the term "Celt" rise to such familiarity and everyday use? The definition of a Celt in the past depended on who was writing and whatever the context was; this means that, today, to describe anything "British" or "Irish" as "Celtic" is incorrect in the historical sense. There is simply too much diversity among these ancient people to group them all together. The Megaws certainly notice the authority in the word "Celt" and are staunch supporters of a sort of "Celtic-power" that seems to be threatened by the likes of Collis, James, and other less-tolerant types— the pair write "we must be on our guard against those who would totally deny a Celtic prehistory". [13] But oddly enough, neither Collis nor James appears to actually detest the modern usage of the word "Celt" - they merely disdain its application to the "early peoples of Britain and Ireland" for which James describes as being too diverse to fall under one name. [14] James goes on to say that "the modern Celts are not the present representatives of a people who have existed continually for millennia, but constitute a true case of 'ethnogenesis'—the birth of an ethnic identity—in *early modern* Europe." [15]

But why and when did this birth occur? And what exactly is an "ethnic identity"? Siân Jones does a good job of answering the latter question when he defines the term as such: "ethnic identity" is "that aspect of a person's self-conceptualization which results from identification with a broader group in opposition to others on the basis of perceived cultural differentiation and/or common descent." [16] The key point here is *self-conceptualization*—ultimately if someone in the modern day perceives themselves as belonging to a particular ethnic group of like-minded individuals then they will, in effect, belong to that group. He or she will probably be asked to defend his or her position at some point in his or her life, but realistically he or she should not have any trouble doing so. The modern Celt may certainly call himself or herself a Celt, but he or she must realize that the modern conceptualization of the term only dates back to the eighteenth century; it is, according to James, a "'reification' of a people that never existed." [17] To say that the Celts never existed may be extreme, but this can be understood to mean that the Celt as it is today did not exist in the past.

As for the former question, it is a good idea to look at the eighteenth century and the rise of colonialism. However, first one must acknowledge Edward Lhuyd. Lhuyd was a Welshman, which is interesting, as "Welsh" is an Anglo-Saxon term given to the Cymry people meaning "foreigner". In the early eighteenth century Lhuyd was busy attempting to organize the family of languages originating in Europe and spreading to the British Isles. In this process he selected the name "Celtic" for a particular branch of the language family tree. [18] The name began to stick to other things, not just the languages, and the people who originally spoke those languages were firmly referred to as Celtic from then on. Lhuyd's selection of the name "Celtic" started a trend that has carried on to this day, particularly in Ireland, Wales, Scotland, and Brittany. In examining the Irish in the eighteenth century it becomes evident that that they were unhappy with their current lot, which involved their being repressed by the British and their having to manage with the potato famine. Having their own Irish national origin myths "proven" through archaeology would have perhaps boosted morale against the Anglo-Protestant English who were then repressing them. [19]

The French, too, were then attempting to use archaeology to reestablish themselves as more powerful people with a reinstated national identity on the European continent. Archaeology could be used to create a sort of "national consciousness." [20] The Emperor Napoleon earlier funded great archaeological digs which then proved to benefit his desire to call upon the Gallic roots of the nation. [21] Later, Napoleon III chose Alésia as the place to honor France's Gallic heritage with a statue. That was the place where the Gaul, Vercingetorix, surrendered to Julius Caesar. To Napoleon III it was "the site both of heroic self-sacrifice by the Gauls in defense of their nation and of the ultimately beneficial, if temporarily painful, victory of Roman 'civilization' over 'barbarism'." [22] In surrendering, Vercingetorix in effect allowed for the creation of a united France. Even today Vercingetorix is seen as one of the top three French heroes according to French children. [23] This connection to the present is an incredibly important one to make, and it is the one sensible conclusion that the Megaws reach. They write,

To ask "Who were the English?" is tantamount to querying the very basis of British national self-identity today. In a multiracial world it surely behoves the English and those who spring from or have been influenced by the English, to debate and seek to understand the make-up of their own particular sense of group identity. Such questions underlie what we think and what we are, and they are relevant far beyond an insular context. [24] [DMD1]

The French are seeking their historical identity, as are the English, as is the rest of the world. Always one looks to the past for answers in the present, and sometimes questions of ethnicity can be answered.

Simon James wrote in 1999 that "Ethnicity is a cultural construct, and may have little to do with the 'real' historical background(s) of the individuals and sub-groups concerned." [25] Siân Jones wrote two years earlier that "ethnic identity is based on shifting, situational, subjective identifications of self and others, which are rooted in ongoing daily practice and historical experience, but also subject to transformation and discontinuity." [26] Both of these quotes tie into the idea that some ethnicities, in this case that of the Celts, can be completely modern fabrications—but there is nothing wrong with this as long as these fabrications are not used to serve an evil purpose. The Nazis exemplify this abuse. It is therefore important to remember, in the words of James, that "we create history...History is what we think, say, and write about the evidence for the past." [27] Evidence may not always be analyzed correctly, but piecing together ancient worlds is a process of growing and learning. Facts should not be omitted or altered to suit political or personal agendas—neutrality is key. With this in mind, the next chapter takes a look at when Roman Britain actually became "Roman". The exact year is highly debatable, for reasons that will be explained ahead.

Chapter Three

The Beginnings Of Roman Britain

When Claudius invaded Britain in 43 CE, what he found there in terms of structure was probably more familiar than the average scholar would expect him to have found, given the failed nature of previous Roman invasions: Julius Caesar's invasions in 55 and 54 BCE were more like reconnaissance missions than anything else; Emperor Augustus' planned invasions were cancelled in 34, 27, and 25 BCE; and, finally, three years prior to Claudius' success, Caligula's men famously gathered seashells on the shore after failing to cross the English Channel. David Mattingly, an archaeologist and historian specializing in the ancient Roman world, wrote, "Even before the Roman conquest, Britain was being drawn into a new cultural milieu centered on Rome." [28] This notion of a "new cultural milieu" taking place before Claudius' invasion challenges the common idea that a "Roman Britain" did not begin until after just such an invasion.

According to Dr. John Creighton, "there was an extent to which certain Britons were becoming Roman without knowing it. This provided the infrastructure of values and ideas amongst the political elite of southeast Britain by the time of the Claudian annexation." [29] Mattingly agrees with Creighton: "Parts of Britain were already embarked on a path of convergence with Rome, long before the British peoples were fully aware of Rome's existence." [30] In effect, Roman Britain certainly existed before Claudius landed on Britain's shores, and it may even have begun to exist in the form of a friendly kingdom before Julius Caesar's invasions precipitated by the island's associations and trading with Gaul, then another part of the Roman Empire.

One must remember that Caesar had attempted to conquer the island's inhabitants in 55 and 54 BCE, nearly a century before Claudius, but even then the Britons had been trading with Gaul—then influenced by Rome—for quite some time. Malcolm Todd, another historian and archaeologist, made an interesting conjecture about Caesar and his prior knowledge of the British Isles before his invasions:

He was fully aware of the long-standing relationships between southern Britain and northern Gaul, which went back at least to the rule exercised by Diviciacus on both sides of the Channel in the earlier first century BC. He would also have known about trade connections between the continent and the island, which were not confined to the Channel narrows. He admitted to seeking intelligence from traders about the peoples of Britain, their institutions, warfare, and ports which might accommodate an invasion fleet, but claimed that he found little of use from this source...Caesar's Gaulish informants could have told him much about the southern British tribes; traders would have known a good deal about markets and harbours. Caesar was intent on portraying his expedition of 55 as a venture into an unknown and dangerous land. Bold as his enterprise was, Caesar was probably as well informed about Britain as any Roman could have been at the time. [31]

This is all a very intriguing line of thought, given the persistent image of Caesar venturing across the channel to the wild lands, the "land of mystery" and mist, when in reality Rome's grip on its territories made the world seem to be a much smaller place. [32] "When the Roman empire erupted into northern Gaul in 57 BC," wrote Mattingly, "this introduced an alien world of status ideas and possibilities to Gallic and British societies." [33] In small ways, such as the adoption of certain "cultural symbols" like wine, feasting, and drinking, Iron Age Britain began to resemble Gaul, which in turn had begun to resemble Rome. [34] Ways of farming and keeping livestock had begun to change. Others like to claim that hill-fortresses, the once archetypal living space and means of organization of the British social structure, disappeared because the Romans made the Britons "abandon their hill-fortresses and move to new towns in the valleys," but "it is clear that in some areas this had already occurred before the Roman occupation, while in others it did not occur till considerably later, if at all." [35] When one considers that southern and southeastern Britain was more likely to be influenced by Gaul and Rome this makes sense: it is a simple matter of geography. But just as there was not one "single 'Roman' identity" there was not one single "British" identity either. [36]

In the words of Mattingly, "The Romans brought towns, roads, stable government, the villa economy, art, culture, literacy, togas, baths and other elements of high culture"; by using the same lens of stereotyping one could categorize the Britons as "semi-naked, spiky-haired, tattooed and woad-painted barbarians, subsequently raised up by the experience of Rome to enjoy the benefits of civilization." [37] This was not entirely accurate, especially considering the fact that many sons of British kings were fostered in Rome well before the time of Caesar's invasion. [38] It was perhaps even common to see British youths in Rome. Todd wrote on fostering and the concept of "friendly kingdoms": "Britain had been made virtually a part of the Roman realm by British rulers who had sent embassies to Augustus and gained his friendship…" [39] The Claudius argument regarding the Romanizing of Britain and the beginning of "Roman Britain" is viewed as largely invalid now because of this fostering. There was apparently more give and take in the Britons' relationship with Rome than one would generally think—"both sides benefited from the association." [40] It was even possible that "kingdoms and provinces can…appear almost interchangeable, and this is reflected in similarities between the roles of governors and monarchs." [41] Given the parallels between the two types of rulers, it is therefore imperative that one must be careful with the use of the word "Romanizing" to begin with. As Mattingly puts it,

Romanization tends to reduce the question of cultural identity to a simple binary opposition: Roman and native. The fact that much of what we identify as "Roman" culture in provinces like Britain in fact came from other provinces in northern and western Europe, rather than from Italy or even the Mediterranean region, should give us pause for thought. Moreover, attention has been drawn increasingly to the infinitely varied nature of the Roman cultural package found around the empire. Regionality and diversity should be just as important in our analysis as elements of homogeneity, but the Romanization paradigm is an obstacle to exploring these. [42]

Some of the influence came from Gaul; some came from Rome by way of Gaul. Also, it is too simple to say that immediately after Claudius' invasion the Britons abandoned their own practices in favor of Roman ones: the archaeological evidence proves otherwise.

Coins are particularly significant from an archaeological perspective because they can be found in relative abundance and they vary under different rulers. For example, in the middle of the first century CE [DMD2] there is evidence of the first dynastic coinage in Britain: old imagery was replaced with Roman likenesses. This has lead Creighton to believe that "something of genuine political significance had happened" at this time to bring about such a change in the imagery. [43] One piece of evidence that supports this theory is the fact that the name "Commios" has been found on coins in Britain. An ally of Caesar, a one Commius was situated in Gaul for a time. He may have found his way to Britain and ruled a kingdom there—this would explain the existence of the name on the coins. [44] Another difference between predynastic coins and dynastic coins is that gold was being measured out in exact quantities in the latter group:

this makes for a noticeable difference in the coloring of the coins when they are shown next to each other. Also of importance is the fact that predynastic and dynastic coins were not found in the same piles, which indicates that the predynastic coins may have actually been taken out of circulation first. [45] Salway wrote, "It is now becoming clear that there was a major change late in the pre-Roman Iron Age in Britain, at least in these densely populated agricultural river-valleys. The Roman Conquest accelerated the development of this new way of life, rather than initiated it." [46]

After the proposed time of Commius, "after about 23 BC, and certainly before 16, Britain was no longer a serious objective of Roman policy or even a subject for propaganda. But diplomatic relations were maintained, if only to make secure the Channel coast of Gaul." [47] The real fear, it seemed, was that Britain was "acting as a refuge for dissident Gauls" and was "supplying help for Gallic revolts." [48] Even so, Caesar remained suspiciously quiet about the real reason(s) behind his invasions several decades earlier. Indeed, "no classical writer discusses at any length the Roman motives for the invasion", and Dudley and Webster go on to say that "The fact is significant: it was not thought to require elaborate justification," but there is more to the situation than this; perhaps Caesar just wanted to hide his true motives in case of failure, which he seems to have experienced. [49] Caesar did lay the groundwork for a new British addition to the Roman Empire, though if one is going to believe Creighton when he discusses the importance of fostering children in Rome with regards to the creation of a "friendly kingdom" which bordered the empire and had good relations with Rome, then perhaps more credit should be given to those emperors who fostered British children before the time of Caesar. Historically, however, the date that marks the beginning of British Rome has usually been selected as the invasion of Caesar: "…while the invasion under Claudius of the southeast was clearly important, the broader shifts in the nexus of power in Britain have much earlier origins. The kings, who held dominion from Caesar's visit until the Flavian period, were fundamental to this change and were in many ways partners in the creation of Roman imperial culture." [50]

Still, Caesar's contact may have just been seen to have hastened a process already well under way: "Close contact between high-ranking Britons and northern Gaul had presumably been current sine the time of Diviciacus' reign before the arrival of Caesar. The big change would come with their successors, the second generation of rulers…This is what happened: a generation after Caesar we see a significant increase in imported 'Roman' material culture in southeast Britain." [51] [DMD3] People simply become fixated on numbers because that is how they categorize and analyze past situations. Mattingly sums the situation up quite well when he says:

Indeed, the Roman conquest of AD 43 is often presented as the end of the Iron Age in Britain, in much the same way as 1066 is held to mark the end of Anglo-Saxon England. This is wrong in several respects. Many of the islands of the British archipelago did not become part of the Roman empire in 43; some never did...Conversely, of course, neither does the year 43 mark the start of civilization and history in Britain. We must recognize that this is a date of convenience for historians and archaeologists... [52]

Such historians and archaeologists should, however, consider the fostering of British noble children to facilitate friendly relations a sign that Britain was well on its way to becoming a part of the Roman Empire before Claudius' successful invasion in 43 CE. The contact the Isle had with Rome before the invasion facilitated some of the relatively peaceful blending of British and Roman religions, as the next chapter examines.

Chapter Four

Religion And Blending Culture In Roman Britain

It can be highly challenging to make inferences about ancient religions, particularly in situations where there is only archaeological evidence available. In the words of Miranda Green, "any attempt at an explanation of Celtic religion must at best be extremely speculative – a construction rather than a reconstruction." [53] She, like many other scholars, is determined to tread lightly, even—or perhaps especially—in instances where there is actual written evidence of religious practices in Britain directly from Romans themselves. Religious practices during the time of Roman Britain did have a distinctly Roman flavor, but whether or not this is because of Gaul's influence from before 43 CE is unclear. [54] What is important is that one can determine what constitutes Roman religion and then compare those findings to those in Britannia so that differences can be spotted between the two.

The majority of these differences become apparent even under casual observation. According to Green,

In terms of religion, ways of expressing the supernatural world became solidified, codified into a grammar of behaviour, attitude and currency of expression many of whose elements shared a generic commonality with Gaul, the Rhineland, Iberia and, indeed, with Italy itself. Such currencies included formalized sacred architecture, the naming of deities and worshippers in inscriptions, and the use of formulaic, repetitive iconography, serving as a visual language of religious identification. All of these features came ultimately from Rome. [55]

With these three currencies—architecture, inscriptions, and iconography—one can attempt to piece together religion in Roman Britain. Because of the lack of an abundant written record in Britannia, it is especially important to examine artwork and architecture in order to gain a better understanding of religious practices there. Green wrote in 1986,

a representative style did not fully develop until the period of Roman rule which stimulated figural portrayal, albeit largely ignoring the 'heavy hand of Roman classicism'. Romano-Celtic stone iconography, influenced by Roman art-formulae but exhibiting religious forms and themes alien to the Mediterranean world, demonstrates that before the conquest there must have existed local and tribal gods, each with a name...and each with specific qualities. [56]

These tribal and local gods must have been named verbally before the Romans came to Britain, as it is hard to picture the island inhabitants coming up with names for their deities only after the arrival of the Romans. [57] Green recognized "about 400 god-names" [58] in the epigraphic record while Cunliffe was more cautious in recognizing over 200. [59] Both agree, however, that certain deities could have more than one name, which would drastically reduce the number of deities in the catalogue.

There are many instances of "twinning," or the double-naming of deities. Sulis Minerva is one such example of this, and it has been suggested that the Celtic name came first to portray dominance or signal that Sulis was at the particular location—*Aquae Sulis*, the sacred spring in Bath—before the Roman Minerva ever arrived. [60] Even though the bronze head of the goddess that can be viewed at the Roman Bath today is in the classical style, Sulis is distinctly British according to the inscriptions that have been found. Minerva, on the other hand, came from Rome and was most likely paired with Sulis because of the belief in their shared healing capabilities. [61] Also at Bath are examples of iconography that are more British than Roman. There is, for example, a portrayal of three female deities who may or may not be the *Suleviae*, a group of triple goddesses. [62] Three seems to have been an important number in Celtic religion, and the triple goddesses crop up quite a bit.

In addition to twinning, there are instances of "divine couples" such as Mercury and Rosmerta, who present a unique blend of Roman and British religious culture. [63] Green pointed out that the female deity in these couples usually keeps her Celtic name while the male stays Roman, as is the case with the example above. [64] Going back to Bath, there is another interesting type of marriage taking place iconographically. There is a Gorgon-esque face sculpted for the front of the temple, only this Gorgon is distinctly male with a wild beard. He is not Medusa but, suggests Green, "transgendered and incorporating the solar and aquatic symbolism of the shrine with the *gorgoneion* of Minerva's breastplate." [65] Solar symbolism in the form of circles and wheels was present in Gaul and Britain long before Rome ever reached those lands. [66] Martin Henig suggests that this intriguing piece of iconography stems from an "Imperial cult," however. In his opinion this unidentified figure is not some sort of British god with Medusa hair—he says it is Neptune. [67] If Sulis Minerva is the double name of the goddess of the spring, though, then it should not be too big a stretch to think that this sculpture could be purposely blending Roman and British characteristics together to form one unique entity.

Also at Bath are the curse tablets, or inscriptions on small sheets of lead that were then folded and thrown into the spring. They are very humanizing: one person, for example, wished to curse whoever stole his cloak. Henig writes of these tablets: "Although, at first glance, they look like an aspect of Celtic cult, in fact the concept of making a contract with a deity, in which one asks the god to do something and promises payment if the act desired is done, comes from the realm of Roman law. The language is very precise and legal and matched by contracts in the secular world." [68] So here is an instance of a tradition that had become popular in Britannia that was probably wholly, if not entirely, Roman.

In terms of architecture, the Roman style of temple is unmistakable. There are a number of examples of wooden temples in Britain that predate Roman ones, though, such as Worth in Kent, Frilford in Oxfordshire, Muntham Court in Sussex, and Haddenham in Cambs. [69] There is also the Hayling Island Temple which is a distinctly Romano-Celtic structure. This means that it consists of a *cella*, as in the Roman style, with an ambulatory around it. This is some more proof of the blending of Roman and Celtic religious practices.

Interesting to note is the extent to which Romans commented on the Druid class and their veneration of forests. Supposedly there were a number of sacred groves associated with the Druids in Britain and on the continent, but it is impossible to recreate the rituals that would have been performed within them without textual descriptions of the procedures themselves. Seeing as the Druids purportedly spent decades memorizing their oral history and rituals, nothing tangible remains for archaeologists and historians to study. What we are left with, then, are Roman accounts of the Druids. The Druids were a particularly interesting group in that they prove to some extent just how important a role religion played in society in the British Isles before the Roman invasion. They were not all-powerful as they are sometimes portrayed, however. In Green's 1986 book she determined that the Druids were "dependent upon tribal chiefs in terms of status and supports"; therefore, with Romans infiltrating the upper echelons of society the "national influence" of the Druids would have been diminished. [70]

One of the Druid practices, human sacrifice, was particularly troubling to the Romans: "the distaste of classical authors for human sacrifice is evident from their writings (though it was not so many centuries since it was practised in the Mediterranean world)." [71] The goal in the Roman's writing about the Druids must have been to further alienate the isle's natives from the rest of the population. Talking about the many kinds of sacrifice certainly would have done just this. Lucan, a Roman, wrote on two Celtic deities and the human sacrifices required to appease them. One preferred drowning, one preferred burning—Cunliffe goes into detail about the names of the gods, but it is difficult to gain a full understanding of the deities and why their worship necessitated human sacrifice based on name meanings alone. [72]

When it comes to understanding religion in Roman Britain there are many challenges a scholar must face along the way. It can be hard to differentiate between British and Graeco-Roman things because of the ties between the two places even before Claudius' formal invasion. Also, Gaul influenced Britain too, especially in the way of burials (though Gaul itself was previously influenced by Rome). While excarnation, or defleshing, was a common practice for a long period of time, there are a number of burial sites in southeastern England that are remarkably similar to those found in Gaul. [73] While Jane Webster would say that "foreign gods were not simply viewed in terms of the Roman pantheon" and that "they were converted to it by force," perhaps religious blending was less harsh than that. [74] Evidence seems to show that the Romans were remarkably tolerant of Celtic deities, as proven by the double-naming and the marriages between Celtic and Roman gods and goddesses. Still, this is not to say that everything was peaceful between the two groups. On the contrary, the various uprisings, rebellions, and physical walls should show otherwise. And it only got worse from the end of the second century onward with the addition of Christianity to the mix.

Chapter Five

The Bitter End

During the reign of Commodus, the Picts breached Hadrian's Wall in 180 CE and killed the governor of Britannia. His replacement, Ulpius Marcellus, won new peace with the Picts, but he faced a vicious mutiny from his men. Supposedly he was too strict, and he only just made it back to Rome alive. The mutiny continued, and when Commodus died, Rome was faced once more with civil war. The pillars of Roman control were beginning to crumble.

The forerunning candidate for position of Emperor was named Septimus Severus, and he set out immediately to disable his enemies. Clodius Albinus, the new governor of Britannia after Marcellus, foresaw the cunning nature of Severus, and sailed to Gaul to meet him in 195 CE. By February of 196 Severus finally joined Albinus at Lugdunum (present-day Lyon, France) and defeated the British governor soundly. Albinus committed suicide not long after, and Severus went on to become Emperor of Rome.

Pretty early on it was determined that three legions were necessary to preserve order in Britannia. This provided the perfect opportunity for power-hungry leaders like Albinus to go crazy with their forces. However, removing the legions to fight elsewhere was a very risky maneuver to take. If all three legions were needed to maintain security and stability on the Isle, then taking even one away provided adequate weakness and enabled the tribes to strike back at the empire. The Scots and Picts were as rowdy as always under Severus, even when he created Britannias Superior and Inferior—one to the south and one to the north.

Emperor Gallienus in the third century faced numerous setbacks during his rule, not least of which being the succession and creation of the "Gallic Empire" from 259-274 CE by the attempted usurper Postumus. Britannia fell into this new Empire until Emperor Aurelian was able to reunite everyone again. Later on in that century, the Diocletian Reforms created more provinces: Britannia Prima, Britannia Secunda, Flavia Caesariensis, Maxima Caesariensis, and Valentia. Even with more governors and smaller provinces, though, nothing could stop the conspiracies of the early 300s CE.

Aptly named the Barbarian Conspiracy (because it involved the Saxons, Scoti, and Attacotti groups) and the Great Conspiracy (which started with mere garrison dissention) this period of tribulation nearly undid all recent progress made by the Romans in Britannia on a small scale, as well as to the Empire at large. The Battle of Adrianople in 378 CE on the continent of Europe may have removed troops or even entire legions from Britannia again, thus allowing the natives to stir themselves up even more. The fourth century brought even more barbarian attacks to the mainland and Isles alike. It would appear that the end of the Roman Empire was drawing nearer every year.

By 383 CE, Roman leaders and troops were removed from western and northern Britannia. Generally it is admitted that by 410 CE Britannia belonged to Rome no longer, as Constantine III—a soldier who declared himself Holy Roman Emperor in 407 CE—had taken with him most of what remained of the military on the island when he moved to Gaul.

Conclusion

With all the struggles facing the Romans in terms of distance from Rome, greedy governors, and unhappy native tribes it is a wonder sometimes that anything got done at all. Roads, aqueducts, sewage systems, baths, and major cities still stand from this time. The capital of Britannia, Londinium (London), is still the capital of Great Britain today, as its foundations were truly laid by the Romans.

Francis Haverfield was the first to use the term "Romanization" in his 1905 book on the subject of Roman Britain. He defined it, according to Jane Webster, as "the means by which non-Romans were 'given' a new language, material culture, art, urban lifestyle, and religion." [75] Since then, the word has been used to present a view of the dichotomous, spontaneous process of acculturation that focused on the elites of what was considered to be 'Roman' society (the concept of what it means to be Roman will be discussed later as well). Romanization is more complex than many scholars give it credit for, and ideally the word would be replaced altogether. [76] But what would it be replaced with then? Webster has adopted the use of the term "Creolization" to account for cultural changes at all levels of Roman society. With this approach she is has taken a debatably more inclusive look at the way Romans and non-Romans should be discussed in society today.

Roman culture has been stood on a pedestal in the Western world since the Renaissance movement of the fourteenth century. Ray Laurence in his article from 1999 quoted P.W. Freeman: "Our view of Roman material culture reflects a Renaissance artistic taste and the creation of a Classical ideal—hence 'Romanization' can be seen to be a construct based on this view of Roman culture, and such a view could not have existed in the Roman past itself." [77] Undoubtedly Freeman was talking about the Renaissance, but also the Neoclassical movement which started in the eighteenth century and rose to prominence along with European imperialism. That Italy, and thus the heart of the ancient Roman world, was part of Europe certainly seemed to affirm the notion that Europe and Europeans were superior to their colonial acquisitions. Europe perceived itself to be "the heir to the civilization of the classical world." [78] It is also important to note as Hingley pointed out that "'civilization' and Western origins are, effectively, used as an excuse and justification for the imperial domination that Western powers exercise over others". [79] This "classical world", however, this root of Western "civilization", was not as homogeneous as Haverfield and his like would have us believe, however.

One tends to forget that, as Greg Woolf wrote, "there was no standard Roman civilization against which provincial cultures might be measured. The city of Rome was a cultural melting pot and Italy experienced similar changes to the provinces. Nor did Romanization culminate in cultural uniformity throughout the empire." [80] He goes on to write, "'Roman' culture itself drew on Greek, Etruscan and other Italian roots, and the iron age cultures of Gaul had included elements drawn from Britain, Germany and Spain as well as from contacts with Mediterranean societies." [81] This is significant, because how can one attempt to define "Romanization" if first one cannot even honestly define what it is to be "Roman"?

Haverfield was not troubled by this question of Roman-ness, however. To him, Romans had a clear, strong identity and therefore the process of Romanization was equally strong and clear-cut through a trickle-down effect. [82] Millett provided a similar model to Haverfield's through several different steps, the main aim being "to administer through the native elite." [83] It is worth going through the steps he gives in order to better understand the other side of the argument. According to Millett, after Roman invasions Roman rule was carried out by the native elites, and "this settlement gave the elite power to govern provided that it was exercised in broad accordance with Roman principles with a Roman style constitution"; there was no forcing of Roman culture on these elites because, supposedly, "the maintenance of their power within society was sufficient incentive in itself"; the elites then adopted "status indicators" in the form of the emulation of "Roman material culture"; and lastly, "progressive emulation of this symbolism further down the social hierarchy was self-generating encouraging others in society to aspire to things Roman, thereby spreading the culture." [84] This is clearly similar to Haverfield's trickle-down approach, but there again, what does it mean to be "Roman"? Woolf attempted to define the Roman culture by saying that it "includes characteristic styles of pottery, building materials and costume; particular beliefs about the dead…and notions about education; customs such as baking bread…building stone monuments…and competing with one's neighbors through Latin declamations, rather than on the battlefield." [85] But even among these there must be slight regional variations in the way things are done.

One finds a similar problem in the more recent past by attempting to define "Creole" culture in the Americas and the Caribbean, as Webster points out in her article. The definition is not as simple as stating that one dominant culture overtook a less-dominant one, nor is it exactly the precise blending of two or more cultures together into one. There is also the term presented by Simon James, and that is "Gallicization." [86] Gallicization, though it points to how "the lowland aristocracies of Britain were 'networked' into the empire through their longstanding ties of kinship, clientage and alliance with the Gallic nobility," also indicates another model of an ancient Britain that is "dependent on continental developments." [87] If adopted, the term Gallicization would shift the focus from Rome to Gaul, but the idea behind Romanization would still be the same—there would still be two culture groups vying for dominance, with the stronger one winning out over the barbaric other. It is important to note what Webster wrote on Romanization: "All models of Romanization thus lead us to the same place: a polarized provincial world of Romans (or Romanized natives) and natives, with no gray areas in between." [88] Creolization complicates this dualistic approach that is understood through both Romanization and Gallicization.

Webster defines Creolization as "a linguistic term indicating the merging of two languages into a single dialect [that] denotes the processes of multicultural adjustment (including artistic and religious change) through which African-American and African-Caribbean societies were created in the New World." [89] Though the term originally had a New World application, that does not mean it cannot be applied to the Old World as well. Webster's goal in her 2001 article was to examine how and to what extent those of low social status were affected by Romanization. [90] This is directly opposite what Haverfield studied at the turn of the century: he believed that "the lowlands, the towns, and...the upper classes" were more Romanized than the "peasantry." [91] More along her lines is the work of Collingwood, who suggested a kind of hybrid acculturation similar to Creolization. The difference between her theory and Collingwood's, however, is that the "fusion processes" of Roman and British culture for Collingwood were studied "in isolation from the consideration of power (that is, an acknowledgement of the fundamental inequalities of the relationship between the colonizer and the colonized)." [92] Avoiding the discussion of power and who holds it is something that cannot be done if one is to fully embrace the term Creolization.

To Webster, "the syncretisms developed by modern creole communities are a balancing act, in which the complex relationship between power and identity is always to the fore." [93] Creolization is not the complete domination of one culture over another, although one culture always invariably exerts power over another to some extent. One example of how Creolization can be understood materially is through the examination of "Celtic"—a loaded word, especially in this instance—and Roman religious iconography. Webster discusses three deities altogether, but Epona in particular due to the fact that the goddess was widespread and had great longevity.

The depiction of Celtic gods in the western provinces was neither a simple emulation of metropolitan art, nor—at the other extreme—a visual expression of nativist opposition to Rome. Rather, as it came into being by negotiating a spiritual pathway between acceptance and resistance, much post-conquest iconography represented a creole art form. Unfortunately, Romanization of form (the use of anthropomorphic imagery) has blinded us to what these icons meant to the people who fashioned and used them. Creolization, as a way to model these complex processes, allows us to reevaluate these images as the active material culture through which new social identities were forged. [94]

Epona was something not wholly Roman and not wholly Celtic, but rather a Romano-Celtic entity through much tribulation. [95] One cannot imagine that the switch in Britain from "Celtic" deities to Roman ones would have happened extremely quickly, either. Creolization could make more sense than Romanization when one considers the inevitable power struggle that was bound to have happened when new religious figures were introduced to the non-Roman populations. Creolization also draws the focus away from the elite and potentially "to other social categories; the urban poor, the rural poor, and that technically most invisible of social groups in the ancient world, the enslaved." [96] There is still much to be done in the way of bringing their histories to the fore. However, Creolization definitely refers more to blending of language than it does to blending of culture as a whole.

The study of Roman Britain is ever-evolving, as odd as that may seem, as new discoveries come to the forefront every year. One can bicker about the implications of language and culture all day long, but the impressive physical works left behind by the Roman Empire that still stand today, millennia later, are truly sights to behold. It would seem that Rome's tendrils did put out roots after all

Bibliography

Aldhouse-Green, Miranda. "Gallo-British Deities and Their Shrines." *A Companion to*
   Roman Britain. ed. Malcolm Todd. Blackwell Publishing, 2004. *Blackwell*
   Reference Online . Web.
   <http://www.blackwellreference.com/subscriber/tocnode.html?id=g97806312182
   34_chunk_g978063121823415>.
BBC History. "Native Tribes of Britain." 2014. Web.
   <http://www.bbc.co.uk/history/ancient/british_prehistory/iron_01.shtml>
Blagg, Thomas and Martin Millet. "Introduction." *The Early Roman Empire in the West.*
   Oxford: Oxbow Books, 2002. 1-6. Print.
Collis, John. "Celtic Myths," *Antiquity* 71.271 (1997): 195-201. *Antiquity.* Web. 22 Jan
   2014.   <
   http://antiquity.ac.uk/ant/071/Ant0710195.htm>.
Collis, John. *The Celts: Origins, Myths and Inventions.* Stroud: Tempus, 2003. Print.
Creighton, John. Coins and Power in Late Iron Age Britain. Cambridge, UK:
   Cambridge University Press, 2000. *Ebrary.* Online.
Creighton, John. Britannia: The Creation of a Roman Province. Oxon: Routledge, 2006.
   Print.

Cunliffe, Barry. "10. Religious Systems." *The Ancient Celts*. Oxford: Oxford University
Press, 1997. 183- 210. Print.

Dietler, Michael. ""Our Ancestors the Gauls": Archaeology, Ethnic Nationalism, and the
Manipulation of Celtic Identity in Modern Europe," *American Anthropologist*
96.3 (1994): 584-605. JSTOR. Web. 21 Jan 2014. <http://www.jstor.org/stable/682302>.

Dudley, Donald Reynolds and Graham Webster. *The Roman Conquest of Britain.*
London: B.T. Batsford, 1965. Print.

Green, Miranda. *The Gods of the Celts.* Totowa, N.J.: Barnes and Noble Books, 1986.
Print.

Henig, Martin. *Religion in Roman Britain.* London, Batsford: 1984. Print.

Henig, Martin. "Roman Religion and Roman Culture in Britain." *A Companion to*
Roman Britain. ed. Malcolm Todd. Blackwell Publishing, 2004. *Blackwell Reference Online.* Web. <http://www.blackwellreference.com/subscriber/tocnode. html?id=g9780631218234_chunk_g978063121823416>

Hingley, Richard. Globalizing Roman Culture: Unity, Diversity, and Empire. Oxon:
Routledge, 2005. Print.

James, Simon. The Atlantic Celts: Ancient People or Modern Invention? London: British
Museum Press, 1999. Print.

James, Simon. "'Romanization' and the Peoples of Britain." *Italy and the West:*
Comparative Issues in Romanization . eds. Simon Keay and Nicola Terrenato.
Oxford: Oxbow Books, 2001. 187-207. Print.
Jones, Siân. The Archaeology of Ethnicity: Constructing Identities in the Past and
Present . London: Routledge, 1997. Print.
Laurence, Ray. "Theoretical Roman Archaeology." *Britannia* 30 (1999): 387-390.
JSTOR . 19 Feb 2014. Web. <http://www.jstor.org/stable/526691>.
Mattingly, David. An Imperial Possession: Britain in the Roman Empire. London:
Penguin, 2007. Print.
Megaw, J. V. S. and M. R. Megaw. "Ancient Celts and Modern Ethnicity," *Antiquity*
70.267 (1996): 175-81. *Antiquity*. Web. <http://antiquity.ac.uk/ant/070/Ant0700175.htm>.
Megaw, J. V. S. and M. R. Megaw. "The Mechanism of (Celtic) Dreams?: a Partial
Response to Our Critics," *Antiquity* 72.276 (1998): 432-5. *Antiquity*. Web. <http://antiquity.ac.uk/ant/072/Ant0720432.htm>.
Millet, Martin. "Romanization: Historical Issues and Archaeological Interpretation."
The Early Roman Empire in the West. Oxford: Oxbow Books, 2002. 35-40.
Print.

Mullen, Alex. "Roman Britain Lecture 1." Oxford University, Oxford. 21 Feb 2014.

Lecture.

Reece, Richard. "Romanization: A Point of View." *The Early Roman Empire in the*

West . eds. Thomas Blagg and Martin Millet. Oxford: Oxbow Books, 2002. 30-

34. Print.

Salway, Peter. *Roman Britain.* Oxford: Oxford University Press, 1981. Print.

Todd, Malcolm. "The Claudian Conquest and Its Consequences." *A Companion to*

Roman Britain . Oxford: Blackwell, 2004. *Blackwell Reference.* Online.

Webster, Jane. "Creolizing the Roman Provinces." *Archaeological Institute of America*

105.2 (2001): 209-225. *JSTOR.* 19 Feb 2014. Web. <http://www.jstor.org/stable/507271>.

Webster, Jane. "*Interpretatio*: Roman Word Power and the Celtic Gods." *Britannia* 26

(1995): 153-161. *JSTOR.* 4 Mar 2014. Web. <http://www.jstor.org/stable/526874>.

Webster, Jane. "Necessary Comparisons: A Post-Colonial Approach to Religious

Syncretism in the Roman Provinces." *World Archaeology* 28.3 (1997): 324-338.

JSTOR . 4 Mar 2014. <http://www.jstor.org/stable/125022>.

Woolf, Greg. Becoming Roman: The Origins of Provincial Civilization in Gaul.

Cambridge: Press Syndicate of the University of Cambridge, 1998. Print.

---

[1] BBC History, "Native Tribes of Britain."

[2] Simon James, *The Atlantic Celts: Ancient People or Modern Invention? (London: British*
Museum Press, 1999), 20.

[3] V. J. S. and M. R. Megaw, "Ancient Celts and Modern Ethnicity," (*Antiquity* 70.267
(1996): 175-81), 177.

[4] James, 17.

[5] James, 41, 27.

[6] John Collis, "Celtic Myths," (*Antiquity* 71.271 (1997): 195-201), 198-9.

[7] Collis, "Celtic Myths," 199.

[8] John Collis, *The Celts: Origins, Myths and Inventions* (Stroud: Tempus, 2003), 102.

[9] Michael Dietler, ""Our Ancestors the Gauls": Archaeology, Ethnic Nationalism, and the
Manipulation of Celtic Identity in Modern Europe," (*American Anthropologist* 96.3
(1994): 584-605), 585.

[10] James, 26.

[11] Dietler, 585.

[12] James, 40.

[13] V. J. S. and M. R. Megaw, "Ancient Celts," 180.

[14] James, 137.

[15] James, 136.

[16] Jones, xiii.

[17] James, 136.

[18] James, 30, 46.

[19] Jones, 6-7.

[20] Jones, 6.

[21] Dietler, 588.

[22] Dietler, 589.

[23] Dietler, 593.

[24] J. V. S. and M. R. Megaw. "Ancient Celts," 179.

[25] James, 76.

[26] Jones, 13.

[27] James, 33.

[28] David Mattingly, *An Imperial Possession: Britain in the Roman Empire*, (London: Penguin, 2007), 17.

[29] John Creighton, *Britannia: The Creation of a Roman Province*, (Oxon: Routledge, 2006), 161.

[30] Mattingly, 48.

[31] Malcolm Todd, "The Claudian Conquest and Its Consequences," *A Companion to Roman Britain*, (Oxford: Blackwell, 2004), section 1.

[32] Donald Reynolds Dudley and Graham Webster, *The Roman Conquest of Britain*, (London: B.T. Batsford, 1965), 17.

[33] Mattingly, 57.

[34] Mattingly, 56.

[35] Peter Salway, *Roman Britain*, (Oxford: Oxford University Press, 1981), 13.

[36] Mattingly, 16.

[37] Mattingly, 5.

[38] Creighton, *Britannia*, 3.

[39] Todd, section 1.

[40] Creighton, *Britannia*, 16.

[41] Creighton, *Britannia*, 18.

[42] Mattingly, 14-15.

[43] Creighton, *Britannia*, 20.

[44] Creighton, *Britannia*, 22.

[45] Creighton, *Britannia*, 21.

[46] Salway, 15.

[47] Todd, section 1.

[48] Salway, 25.

[49] Dudley and Webster, 51.

[50] Creighton, *Britannia*, 157.

[51] Creighton, *Britannia*, 24.

[52] Mattingly, 47-48.

[53] Miranda Green, *The Gods of the Celts* (Totowa, N.J.: Barnes and Noble Books, 1986), 7.

[54] Miranda Aldhouse-Green, "Gallo-British Deities and Their Shrines," *A Companion to Roman Britain,* ed. Malcolm Todd (Blackwell Publishing, 2004).

[55] Aldhouse-Green.

[56] Green, 12.

[57] Green, 17.

[58] Green, 32.

[59] Barry Cunliffe, "10. Religious Systems," *The Ancient Celts* (Oxford: Oxford University Press, 1997, 183- 210), 184.

[60] Green, 155 and Aldhouse-Green.

[61] Aldhouse-Green.

[62] Aldhouse-Green.

[63] Green, 36.

[64] Green, 36-7.

[65] Aldhouse-Green.

[66] Green, 44.

[67] Martin Henig, "Roman Religion and Roman Culture in Britain," *A Companion to Roman Britain*, ed. Malcolm Todd (Blackwell Publishing, 2004).

[68] Henig, "Roman Religion."

[69] Green,18-9.

[70] Green, 26.

[71] Green, 28.

[72] Cunliffe, 185.

[73] Cunliffe, 179 and Alex Mullen, "Roman Britain Lecture 1," Oxford University, Oxford (21 Feb 2014).

[74] Jane Webster, "*Interpretatio*: Roman Word Power and the Celtic Gods." *Britannia* 26 (1995: 153-161), 160.

[75] Jane Webster, "Creolizing the Roman Provinces." *Archaeological Institute of America* 105.2 (2001: 209-225), 211.

[76] *Richard Hingley, Globalizing Roman Culture: Unity, Diversity, and Empire, (Oxon: Routledge, 2005), 14.*

[77] Ray Laurence, "Theoretical Roman Archaeology," *Britannia* 30 (1999: 387-390), 388.

[78] Greg Woolf, *Becoming Roman: The Origins of Provincial Civilization in Gaul.* (Cambridge: Press Syndicate of the University of Cambridge, 1998), 4-5.

[79] Hingley, 21.

[80] Woolf, 7.

[81] Woolf, 20.

[82] Hingley 34.

[83] Martin Millet, "Romanization: Historical Issues and Archaeological Interpretation," *The Early Roman Empire in the West* (Oxford: Oxbow Books, 2002, 35-40), 38.

[84] Millet, 38.

[85] Woolf, 11.

[86] Simon James, "'Romanization' and the Peoples of Britain," *Italy and the West: Comparative Issues in Romanization*, eds. Simon Keay and Nicola Terrenato (Oxford: Oxbow Books, 2001, 187-207), 190.

[87] James "'Romanization'" 195, 191.

[88] Webster, 216.

[89] Webster, 209.

[90] Webster, 210.

[91] Webster, 211.

[92] Webster, 211.

[93] Webster, 212.

[94] Webster, 223.

[95] Webster, 221.

[96] Webster, 223.

Printed in Great Britain
by Amazon